Asperger Syndrome –
What Teachers Need to Know

Asperger Syndrome –
What Teachers Need to Know

Matt Winter

Written for Cloud 9 Children's Foundation

Jessica Kingsley Publishers
London and Philadelphia

First published in the United Kingdom in 2003
by Jessica Kingsley Publishers
116 Pentonville Road
London N1 9JB, UK
and
400 Market Street, Suite 400
Philadelphia, PA 19106, USA

www.jkp.com

Library of Congress Cataloging in Publication Data
A CIP catalog record for this book is available from the Library of Congress

British Library Cataloguing in Publication Data
A CIP catalogue record for this book is available from the British Library

ISBN-13: 978 1 84310 143 7
ISBN-10: 1 84310 143 2

Printed and Bound in the United States by Thomson-Shore, Inc.

Contents

Introduction

As a primary teacher I understand how valuable a teacher's time is. When I needed to learn about Asperger Syndrome (AS), I discovered that I would have to wade through many substantial books written from a parental or psychological perspective, not from a teacher's point of view. After many hours of reading literature on Asperger Syndrome, talking with parents of children with AS, discussions with professionals, experience as a classroom teacher and experience working with children with AS, I have been encouraged to write this condensed book to help save teachers' time.

The aim of the book is to provide you, the reader, with a summary of the information currently available on AS that is relevant to teachers, and to provide you with a better understanding of your AS students, quick tips and practical ideas that you can start using straight away in your class.

I hope that reading this gives you a good initial grounding and that you will be motivated to pursue further reading on the subject. At the end of the book there is a list of recommended reading and websites that highlight the sources I have found most useful. I hope you find this book valuable.

CHAPTER 1

What is Asperger Syndrome?

Asperger Syndrome is a developmental disorder that falls within the autistic spectrum. It is sometimes referred to as high functioning autism (particularly in the USA), and though it is often suggested that this is a different condition, from a teacher's point of view the two are for practical teaching purposes interchangeable. Asperger Syndrome is characterized by difficulty with four main areas:

1. Social Interaction

2. Communication

3. Imagination (e.g. imagining what others are thinking)

4. Sensory Sensitivity (e.g. to bright light, noise, textures, tastes, touch, smells).

Lorna Wing (Burgoine and Wing, 1983) described the main clinical features of AS as:

• lack of empathy

• naïve, inappropriate, one-sided interaction

- little or no ability to form friendships
- pedantic, repetitive speech
- poor nonverbal communication
- intense absorption in certain subjects
- clumsy and ill-co-ordinated movements and odd postures.

Personally, I believe this puts a very negative spin on the syndrome and I prefer to think of it differently, in a more positive light. Some of the positive traits commonly associated with AS are:

- honesty
- reliability
- dedication
- determination.

Children with AS can also be diagnosed with other syndromes or conditions that occur with Asperger Syndrome. Some common ones are:

Attention Deficit Hyperactivity Disorder (ADHD/ADD) – an inability to maintain concentration, even when trying his or her hardest.

Dysgraphia – difficulty putting thoughts into writing, particularly while trying to read the board or listen to someone talk at the same time.

Dyslexia – difficulty with decoding single words, making reading, writing and spelling difficult.

Dyspraxia or Developmental Co-ordination Disorder (DCD) – a neurologically based impairment or immaturity of the organization of movement. This can affect a person's coordination, making him appear clumsy or unable to write neatly, his language development, his perception and his ability to organize his thoughts.

Echolalia – a tendency to mimic other people's speech.

Nonverbal Learning Disability (NLD) –this term is often used to categorize specific disorders that do not affect speech, Asperger Syndrome being one of them. However, there are people with learning difficulties who do not fit the criteria for currently recognized disorders, and they are then described in general terms as having NLD.

Obsessive Compulsive Disorder (OCD) – a disorder where people develop obsessions and/or compulsions (senseless repetitive actions) that they perform in an effort to reduce discomfort and anxiety. These obsessions and compulsions become all encompassing and intrude on the person's life.

Tourette Syndrome – neurological disorder. Can be motor (e.g. flapping hands), vocal (e.g. making unusual noises, or involuntarily saying inappropriate words), or behavioural (e.g. repeating a task).

Tony Attwood has described AS as a different way of approaching life, one that is dominated by the pursuit of knowledge and truth. The way AS may present itself in your classroom is explored in the next section.

CHAPTER 2

What signs might a child display?

One of the aspects of AS that makes it difficult to get to grips with is that it presents itself in many different ways. No two children with AS will have exactly the same set of symptoms. Below is a list of the possible signs a child with AS might display and the ways in whcih he or she might behave. Keep in mind that each child displays each sign to a different extent, in a different way, and may well not display some at all. The signs may also come in waves – a certain sign might not be prominent for a while but can return later on. They are more likely to become apparent if the child is stressed, anxious or tired.

General

Honest

- Will not understand why people lie.

- Will say exactly what he thinks.

- Will stick loyally by people.

- Learns to lie later than her peers, and when she does will often be an unconvincing liar, often without awareness of the transparency of the lie.

Creative

- Often approaches a problem from a completely different angle from the rest of the class.

- Prefers to use methods that she devises herself to solve problems, rather than conventional methods.

- Can genuinely find it hard to distinguish fiction from reality.

- Is often musical, artistic or dramatic.

Special interests (fascinations/obsessions)

- May develop a topic or couple of topics of special interest.

- May add new special interests from time to time.

- Wants to find out all he can on the current topic.

- May develop special interests in order to help facilitate conversation, indicate intelligence to others, provide order and consistency, but mainly simply because she really enjoys them.

- Can be extremely knowledgeable about topics of special interest and can often communicate about them in an adult way.

- The special interest(s) often can be a "safe zone" as he feels more secure when immersed in his interest.

Enjoys routines

- Responds well to set routines – she likes to know what to expect during the school day.

- Dislikes deviation from routines and may become upset by last minute changes of lesson or teacher.

- Can create many routines of her own to put some order back into her life.

- If there is an order to a routine, she does not like the order to be changed.

Social Interaction

Difficulty reading social cues and body language

- May interrupt conversations at inappropriate times.

- Will not pick up on verbal or nonverbal signals that a person has had enough of the conversation.

- Will often act the same in different social situations (e.g. always very formal) and in the same way to different people (e.g. peers and school principal).

- Can misinterpret polite conversation or greetings as signs of real interest or friendships.

- Is very eager to make friends but appears "socially clumsy".

- Misses the meaning of sarcasm.

- Often misinterprets facial expressions.

- Finds the concept of turn taking difficult to put into practice

High stress levels

- Social and communication difficulties, frequently in addition to sensory difficulties, make large demands on the child and he or she often has high stress levels as a result.

- Particularly when most stressed, may be prone to repeating things over and over.

- Very aware when he has made public errors, and is upset by these but unaware of how to fix them.

- Can quickly become physically and mentally tired as a result of hight stress levels. Often needs a nap or time out to calm down and recharge energy.

Difficulty expressing/modulating his or her emotions

- May get more emotional than situation warrants.

- May appear unmoved when in fact she actually is moved.

- Can have a quick temper.

- Finds it hard to restrain impulsive thoughts or actions.

- May laugh inappropriately when he doesn't understand the situation.

- May express inappropriate emotions (e.g. may laugh in a sad situation, or cry in a happy one).

- May find it difficult to distinguish emotions, e.g. sad from angry.

Difficulty reading other people's emotions

- Will listen to what is said but fails to interpret correctly the facial expression of the person and misses the tone it was said in so only partially understand what is being said.

- May understand that someone else is happy or sad but may not know how to respond appropriately.

Strong moral code and sense of justice

- Has a need for things to be fair.

- Once a value is adopted, she can get upset when other people disregard it so only partially understands what is being said.

- Gets upset when other people ignore rules.

- Class policeman!

Theory of mind difficulties*

- Has trouble working out what another person might be thinking.

- Has difficulty working out a person's motivation.

- Can at times assume, and work on the basis, that everyone thinks and feels the same as he does about things.

- May assume that other people know everything she knows about something.

- Can do things and not realize he is hurting the feelings of someone else.

- May have difficulty with reading comprehension especially involving passages about people.

- Will often completely believe that she is 100 per cent right.

---

* Theory of mind refers to the notion that many individuals with Autistic Spectrum Disorders do not understand that other people have thoughts, ideas, and ways of thinking that are different from theirs. They therefore also have difficulty understanding the attitudes, actions and emotions of others (Edelson 1995).

Controlled play

- Needs to be in control of games.
- Has a tendency to play games that mimic reality.
- Has little interest in games that he does not have complete control of.
- Tends to be happier with noncompetitive games.

Academic

Literal thinking

- Things that the child hears are taken in a very literal sense (e.g. "raining cats and dogs" – will look for the cats and dogs).
- Often fails to grasp implied meaning.

Visual memory

- Tends to remember in pictures and scenes, although language can be his or her best skill.
- Recalls things shown to him more easily then said.
- Finds it very hard to remember the sequence of things that are spoken.

Exceptional long-term memory

- Can recall things (particularly images) from his or her very early years.

- May be able to recall things over a long time span.

- Is often able to list large amounts of factual information.

- May have exceptionally large vocabulary for his age, and a very accurate understanding of the meaning of individual words.

- May have short-term auditory memory problems, especially if also ADD/ADHD.

Difficulty thinking ahead

- Finds it difficult to predict likely outcomes.

- Finds it hard to think through how things will have an effect in the future.

- Finds it hard to choose between options so will tend to make a rash choice or none at all.

- Finds it extremely difficult to predict how people will react.

Rigid thinking

- Has a need for things to be black or white.

- Dislikes ambiguity.

- Will often pursue an unsuccessful problem-solving method rather than change it.

- Has excellent knowledge of the exact meaning of words.

- May often be a high achiever in topics that have a rigid structure to them.

- Loses train of thought if interrupted when speaking or thinking.

- Dislikes change more than other children.

- Dislikes the unexpected.

Difficulty generalizing

- Once a skill is learnt, he or she will not instinctively be able to apply it in a different situation.

Perfectionist

- Has a fear of criticism and of appearing stupid to others.

- Is very sensitive to any criticism.

- Finds failure absolutely crushing.

- Does not like doing something if she may make an error (even in a minor way).

- Particularly dislikes public failures.

- Finds competetive activities very stressful because of perceived potential for social humiliation.

Physical/Senses
Motor clumsiness

- Often has odd gait when walking.

- Has difficulty with tasks that require fine motor skills (e.g. tying shoe laces).

- Often has messy handwriting.

- May find ball sports and balancing activities difficult.

- May become more obviously affected by motor clumsiness in adolescence.

- Tends to dislike and find difficult competitive team sports.

Rhythm

- May have a fantastic ear for rhythm when playing by him or herself.

- May find it very difficult to keep a rhythm with others.

- Finds rhythm both comforting and yet highly frustrating.

Sensory sensitivity

- Often far more sensitive to sensory input than other children.

- May find certain smells, sounds, lights or tastes unpleasant to the point of being torturous.

- May be physically ill when he smells a certain smell or really physically hurt if he is touched.

VISUAL

- Bright light can be unbearable.

- Flickering light can be unbearable.

- May be fascinated by certain lights.

- May find it physically unpleasant to read certain text.

- May dislike being looked at – it has been said "I feel as if the person will see inside me".

AUDITORY

- High pitched, sudden or loud noises can be unbearable or highly distracting.
- May hear things before other people.
- May hear things others don't hear at all or don't notice, e.g. sound of electric light.

TACTILE

- May intensely dislike the feel of some fabrics, especially in clothing.
- May find very unpleasant the feel of labels in clothing.
- May find it painful or unpleasant to be touched, especially on certain areas of the body.
- May be very sensitive to discomfort in clothing.

OLFACTORY

- Strong odours, particularly perfumes, can overwhelm.

- May often be the first to smell something.

- May intensely dislike particular smells.

Poor sense of direction

- Needs lots of visual landmarks included in directions.

- Some children with AS can develop an excellent long-term memory of a place once these landmarks are established. May only need one familiarization visit and will instantly be able to find way next time.

Bilateral co-ordination difficulties

- Finds it hard to move both sides of the body in harmony.

- May as a result find writing and ball skills difficult.

Visual perception difficulties

- Can find it hard to distinguish an object from the background.

- Has difficulty working out proximity of objects.

- Has difficulty identifying distinct differences in similar objects.

- Can find it extremely difficult to look at someone when talking as there is so much visual and aural information to process at the same time.

- May have difficulty going down stairs because of visual disorientation.

Aural perception problems

- May find it difficult to distinguish a noise (e.g. a teacher speaking) from background noise.

- May find it difficult to interpret words as meaningful language.

- May find it difficult to understand what is being said if there are competing sensory stimuli.

High pain threshold

- May not appear not feel low levels of pain.

- May express the feeling of pain through behaviour. For example, if a child has a belly ache, instead of holding her tummy and complaining about it being sore as other children would, she may instead become unusually irritable and uncooperative when you interact with her.

- Can be over and under sensitive to temperature.

CHAPTER 3

What are some strategies for the classroom?

Because every child with Asperger Syndrome is unique, there is no foolproof list of strategies that will work for everyone. Below are some ideas that have been tried and found to be successful with certain children with AS. Choose ones that you think might benefit the child you are working with and give them a go.

You may have implemented many of these strategies in your classroom already. Remind yourself of their particular importance for children with AS. See if you can generalize new strategies for the whole class. Be inventive and keep on trying.

Above all else, maintain consistency in the classroom. These children need plenty of structure and will react negatively to changes. Keep your sense of humour and remember it is OK to have a laugh!

Organization

Create a visual organizer

The ability of children with AS to think in pictures can be used to aid their organization. A common strategy is to use visual organizers in the form of a series of pictures showing the sequence of events or tasks to be done. Exactly how these are created and used depends greatly on the child.

When creating one, first ask yourself what you wish to achieve with it. You may wish to create one that shows the sequences of subjects or events over the whole school day, or perhaps over just one teaching block. You may just wish to break down the tasks that the child needs to do during draft writing, or reading.

Once the purpose has been decided you can think about the physical form the organizer will take. If the child does not like to be singled out then you may want to create a large one that can be used with the whole class. If the child needs more assistance, a personal one that can fit on the top of his or her desk may be more useful.

The next step is to create the pictures that will represent each task or event. Some children may find abstract pictures hard to interpret so photos of the actual objects may work better. For example, if you are doing an organizer for the whole day, you may have a photo of a reading book for reading time or a photo of the computer for information technology. For some children a drawing of a book or a computer may be sufficient. Colour often helps and you should write the word that matches the picture underneath it, e.g. "Reading" under the picture of the book.

The last task in creating the organizer is to attach a piece of Velcro or Blue-Tac to the back of each picture, and to make a strip that the pictures will be attached to. When first using visual organizers, spend time ensuring that the child has made a link between the picture and the activity. Introduce the pictures gradually, one at a time, pulling them out at the beginning of an activity, then putting them away at the end. Continue this until there is a definite link, then progress onto an ordered strip where the pictures are shown one after in the order in which activities will take place.

Once established, make sure that what has been prepared on the organizer is gone over with the student or with the whole class. If you are creating organizers for blocks of time or the whole day it helps to go over them before the class begins so that the child has as much pre-warning as possible. Any changes to the order need be carefully explained before the pictures are swapped around.

Warn about changes

Give the child as much advance warning about changes to the scheduled program as possible. Give her a reason for the change and alter her visual organizer. Talk her through the situation and tell her exactly what will be required. Rehearse any new activity with her if you can.

Lists and schedules

Create lists of tasks to be done. Assign times by which each will be done, so that progress can be monitored.

Colour code

Use colours, and possibly strong visual symbols, to indicate different areas of the classroom, and different activities. The blue shelf may be where maths equipment is kept. The red shelf is where language materials are etc. Make sure the labelling is clear. If possible, extend this throughout the school, so that different areas of the school have different colours or visual codes that are easy to recognise.

Create a school map

If the child is having trouble navigating the school or working out where he is allowed to go, create a colour coded map. Have a certain colour for areas where the child may only go with a teacher's permission or in an emergency. Do not say to him they are areas he "can not go to" as they might take this literally even in extreme situations.

Arrange for an early arrival

If the child is having trouble organizing herself at the start of the day or settling down, arrange for her to arrive at school early. Have a place where she can go (e.g. library) where she can relax and adjust to being at school before heading to class.

Choose seating carefully

One of the most important considerations when choosing where to seat a child with AS is his or her sensory sensitivities. This is covered in a later section of this chapter.

In addition you need to take into account the distractions in different areas of the room. The child should be away from areas where other children are likely to be doing distracting activities such as a mat or art area, or the classroom door. The classroom might need to be rearranged slightly to ensure there are quite separate work and play areas.

Some children might actually prefer to face a wall or a window (so long as the scene outside is not distracting) so they do not notice the other children as much, or you might at least have a desk set up in this way that the child can use if he wants to.

Also think about whether the child has an easy path through to a time out place and to the teacher for help.

Class work

Make everything visual

Remember that many of these children are visual learners. Any visual link you can make will help him or her. There are plenty of books available on visual strategies and visual information organizers for use in the classroom (see the Resources section).

Do things as you talk

The child with AS will often appear to be very inattentive when people are talking. He does not gain much from body language and does not naturally look at people when they are talking. In this case it can actually help him *not* to look at you.

The opposite can also be true. A child with AS might not take in anything you say even if she appears to be looking at you and listening, or she may only pick out certain words or phrases from a conversation.

If you can, do something that is visually interesting while talking relating to what you are talking about. For example use a model or create a diagram. This will encourage the child to look at you and begin to pick up on body language. It will also help him or her remember what you are talking about by tying the concept to something visual which is more easily recalled.

Use his/her special interests

The child's special interests are a huge source of motivation for a child with AS. There are many ways that you can use this to your advantage, including:

- relate the work you are doing to the special interest in some way. For example, if the special interest is airplanes and you are studying time in maths, you could base his work around airline timetables.

- show him that what he is learning will help him when he wants to find out more information about his special interest

- use extra time investigating her special interest as a reward (e.g. when she completes certain activities, she can have ten minutes in the library)

- make use of his special skills to give him status in the class (e.g. if he is big on computers, let him be a computer monitor who helps the other children with computers).

Allow her her own methods

When the child has worked through the problem, get her to explain her method to you. Be prepared to let the child use unconventional techniques and processes, as long as she works.

Use timers

Often a child with AS will have a poor sense of time. Use an egg timer or a similar, easy to follow device to set the amount of time for a task. Point out what he needs to have finished by specific times. If you use this strategy, stick to it. Do not expect him to work past the timer. Praise him when he completes the required work. Encourage him to beat his output from last time. In this way he is working in competition with himself, not with the other children in the class.

Speaking ball

During class discussions, use a ball, stick or other object that gets passed around to the person who is allowed to speak. This will help the child with AS learn to take turns and not interrupt in discussion groups. Explain the reason behind turn taking.

Alternative note taking methods

If the child has difficulty with handwriting, use a variety of methods of note taking. The teacher aide and the student might share the writing, a dictaphone might be used, work could be typed or keywords written to fill in the gaps (i.e. cloze work). Avoid copying from a board where possible. Drafting a piece of work can also be stressful. He may learn more by going straight to writing out the good copy.

Teacher selected groups

Always use teacher selected groups for activities – this ensures that the child will not be left out. Because of their difficulties with social interaction, and with competitive team sport, children with AS are often not amongst the first to be 'picked' by their classmates to join teams or groups.

Cooperative learning strategies

You probably use lots of these in your class already. They are a good way to encourage children to interact. The think, pair, share model is particularly good. The think, pair, share model involves pairing students up during discussions. When posing a question, tell the students to just think about the question and not put their hands up. Give them a full 20 seconds to think then get them to turn to their partner and, one at a time, share their thoughts. Gain their attention back and ask for answers from the class. This model allows for more thinking time and greater participation. Answering the question with their partners often gives children more courage to speak out to the whole class. However, these strategies can also be very threatening to a child with AS because they involve a large amount of one-on-one social interaction. The predictable structure will be appealing though, and as long as you introduce them gradually they should be of real benefit. Chose just one strategy to teach to the class at a time. Use a topic that you know the child with AS will find easy to talk about and use it to practise the strategy before it is used during a lesson. You may also want to teach the strategy to the child before teaching it to the class so that he is more familiar with it.

Be patient when asking questions

When you ask a question, the child has to stop thinking her current thoughts, lock those away for later, decipher the question, formulate an answer and then respond. This may take a while. If you interrupt or try to finish sentences for her, she may have to start her thought processes over again. Don't expect her to look at you, as this may actually break her concentration.

Be directive

Remember that giving a child with AS a choice can be stressful. He can struggle for ages over which is the best choice and a decision means he has to risk getting it wrong. It may seem like a straightforward choice to you but it could feel like the biggest decision in the world for the child. While it is useful for the child to learn about choices, keep them easy and help him through them.

Encourage mistakes

This sounds strange but often children with AS need to learn that it is OK to make mistakes so long as they learn from them. If a child makes a mistake, move the blame away from her. Tell her the task is really hard and you are pleased she is trying it. Say things like, "I am glad you made that mistake because now I know that I need to teach you about... Shall I teach you that now so that you can get it right next time?"

Create a code for help

As children with AS are very insecure about appearing stupid, invent a code that the child can use to ask for help without the other children realizing. He may place his pencil case a certain way on his desk or stretch in a particular way to indicate that he needs help. You can then approach him as if you are looking at his work and give him ideas or the support he is looking for.

Monitor your speech

Check that when giving instructions:

- your voice is the primary sound and is not competing against background noise

- you pause between sentences to allow processing time

- not too much information is given out in one go – only one instruction at a time

- sarcasm or hints at meaning are avoided

- metaphors and other figures of speech are explained

- your instruction is unambiguous

- you only say, "Will you…" and "Can you…" if there actually is a choice.

Repeating instructions

Get children in the class to repeat back the instructions given. Get the child with AS to come to you before going to her desk to repeat back what she is going to do. Follow up with other questions to ensure understanding and that the child is not just parroting information. Other children in the class could also be tasked with repeating instructions to the child before starting their work.

Whispered thoughts

Many children with AS work best when they say their thoughts out loud. If the child in your class does this, do not stop him but encourage him to whisper the thoughts instead.

Arrange an alternative PE program

Due to their poor motor skills and difficulty with social interaction, team sports are a huge challenge for children with AS. Working on one of these two skills is very taxing for the child and working on both at once can be almost impossible. PE then becomes a time of great stress for both the child and the teacher and often very little is achieved. It is usually far more beneficial for the child to do an alternative PE program when you are doing team sports with the class. A rotation of responsible classmates can be trained in two-person PE games that help with motor skills and co-ordination. Later on you could have games that involve two pairs playing against each other. This will help the child to learn about being part of a team in a far less threatening manner. These children can then play the games with the child with AS while the class is playing sport. Most people would perceive there to be a stigma associated with being separated from the class like this but for the child with AS it is usually a great relief and far better than the alternative. Where it is not possible to "rescue" the child with AS in this way and for some reason he needs to be included in team sports, make sure that the teams are selected by the teacher, not by the children in the class.

Home and school communication

Keep the flow of information between home and school open. Consider introducing a notebook that goes home each night with any notes about the day, and back to you in the morning. You can identify a couple of things you are working on in class and have a simple symbol system to indicate progress for that day. For example, you might be working on turn taking in conversations, working at his or her desk, or checking answers. At home, the parent can make a note of anything that is going on (or changing) that might have an effect on the child.

Sensory sensitivity

Auditory

A child's behaviour can be altered by a noise that others, including yourself, do not notice. Tantrums might occur at the same time of day and be linked, for example, back to the caretaker raking leaves. Here are some strategies for dealing with this sensitivity:

- Identify and eliminate, where possible, high pitched continuous noises (e.g. electric motors), and sharp, startling noises. If you are unable to do this, seat the child away from the source of such noises.

- Have a quiet place the child can go and work.

- Let the child wear earplugs to block out distracting background noise.

- Let the child listen to soothing music using a walkman. The music needs to be carefully chosen.

Visual

Some children with AS can be particularly sensitive to light, especially bright or some forms of artificial light. This can make it difficult or even painful for them to concentrate. If this is the case:

- Seat the child where he is not in direct sunlight.

- Avoid fluorescent bulbs where possible. Otherwise, provide a lamp with a standard bulb on his desk.

- Let the child wear sunglasses.

- Get him to cup his hands around his eyes to block peripheral vision if he is becoming overwhelmed.

Tactile

Children with AS often have tactile sensitivities quite unlike those of other children.

- Clothes are often a real issue for children with AS. Talk with the parents to ensure the child is wearing clothes that she is comfortable in.

- It is often useful if the clothes are easy to put on and take off (e.g. Velcro-fastened shoes) especially if the child has difficulty with fine motor skills. Make sure that the child can cope with changes of clothing required during the school day.

- Learn where the sensitive areas of the body are for the child you are teaching. When you touch her it might really hurt even (or for some children, especially) if you only touch lightly!

- Remember that the child may have a very high pain threshold. Remember that the child may have a very high pain threshold. You often need to look for behavioural signs that show she may be hurting, such as increased irritability or sudden uncooperativeness.

Olfactory

Children with AS are often hypersensitive to smell. They can often smell things that other children can't smell, and may find some smells unbearable. You can help to prevent problems with this in the following ways:

- Avoid wearing strong perfumes or aftershaves.

- Allow fresh air to circulate in the class.

- Be aware that anything strong smelling in a class may create a difficulty for a child with AS.

- Allow him or her to bring to class a small item impregnated with a calming smell.

Taste

Children with AS are sensitive to both the taste and the texture of food, and tend to be wary of new things and resistant to change. They are often creatures of habit where food is involved and often prefer to eat the same thing day after day. You can help them with this by adopting the following approach:

- Get the child to taste just a very small amount of something new.

- Be prepared for a negative reaction to new foods.

- Do not push the issue of trying a new food.

School environments and sensory difficulties

Within any environment there are a large number of stimuli. When introducing a child with AS into a new environment, think about the stimuli and decide whether the child will be able to tolerate them. Let him watch the first time and then join in.

School assemblies are a prime example. The crowdedness, action at the front, smell of bodies and intense noise can absolutely overwhelm some children. Often it is better that he has some quiet time during assemblies rather than forcing him into what is a torturous situation. For other children it may be the music lab or technology rooms that prove to be too much. See whether there is a less stressful alternative available.

Anxiety/Tempers

Manage your emotions

Always remember that your response will have a direct influence on any tense situation. If you get angry as well, it will be like throwing petrol on a fire. If you stay calm and speak in a quiet voice, you will be a soothing influence. It doesn't matter how you feel inside, what matters is how you appear. Try and sort out conflicts when you are both calm. Children can't respond well when stressed either.

Stress ball

A stress ball allows the child to squeeze and squash the tension out on the ball. The repetitive squeezing action can also be a calming movement for some children. Koosh balls and other fiddle toys may also help.

Teach anger management

The following methods can be taught to your whole class but will particularly benefit the child with AS:

- Talk through the physical and emotional cues that let us know we are getting angry.

- Stop, Think, Do – Talk the class through this technique to use when getting angry. **Stop** what you are doing, **think** about what you could do and what might happen, choose the option that will keep you safe and **do** it.

- Teach the class how, when you are getting angry, to stop and slowly count to ten.

- Teach deep breathing techniques.

- Give safe alternatives to hitting – if there is a need to destroy, make it productive. Pupils can crush cans for recycling, tear up cardboard boxes so they can be laid flat for the recycling bin, etc.

Safe place

Designate somewhere as a safe area the child can go to if stressed. Make sure it is nearby and actually is safe. If it can't be out of the class then consider using a bean bag or the reading corner. Create some rules for its use regarding the time that can be spent in it. If the child is able to, she should let you know that she is going there. It may be helpful to schedule a regular time for her to visit this place so that she can rest and recharge her batteries. Children with AS need this time out from the stress of dealing with busy classrooms.

Deep pressure therapy

This needs to be discussed with the parents to see whether it works for their child and whether it is appropriate to do it at school. The most common use of it in the classroom is a weighted vest which helps keep some children calm. This can be put on as needed.

Security item

Talk with the parents about a particular item the child finds comforting. For some children it is a piece of cloth that they like to touch, some like something with a particular smell (can also be used to block smells they find hard to cope with), for others it will be something to do with their special interest. The child can carry this with him and use it when he is stressed.

Burning off anxiety

When the anxiety is at a low level, lots of these soothing techniques will be effective. When it is at a high level the child may need to burn it off. This can be done by going for a run or doing some other high energy exercise. Even taking a massage might help. Children with AS respond extremely well to physical activity as a form of stress relief.

Divert attention

If the child starts to get stressed and begins repeating things or gets stuck doing a routine, gently divert her attention to help her save face. Don't get drawn into answering repeated questions over and over.

Notebook of things not understood

Get the child to carry a notebook with him. In it he can jot down anything that he sees, hears or that happens that he doesn't understand. These can be academic issues, social issues or anything of concern. Once a day he can share the notebook with you.

Regular check-ins

It can be useful to schedule a certain time each day where the two of you can chat about things and monitor overall progress. This would be a good time to explain things that are confusing the child or that he is worrying about. A simple distracting activity often eases the pressure of talking in these situations (e.g. colouring-in).

Relevant consequences

When a child with AS does something that is really inappropriate, the consequence must be relevant to what has happened and involve *doing* something rather than just words. Saying sorry has little meaning. If she has taken something belonging to someone else then maybe she should share something of hers. When something has happened, always look back and work out what the precipitant (cause) was. This will help you work out the appropriate consequence. Have a discussion with the child after she has calmed down, about inappropriate and unacceptable behaviours. Use diagrams or other visual aids.

Pick your battle

Work on those behaviours that are unacceptable. The child will probably have other behaviours that many will label as odd – don't worry about these if they are not having a negative consequence. Choose the battles you need to win.

Reward systems

All children respond strongly to reward systems and can be particularly effective for children with AS who have such a keen sense of fairness and a very strong need to achieve. However, systems based on intrinsic rewards have much less effect on children with AS than they do on other children. Therefore, when designing the reward system, try to set it up so that the child is earning something tangible. Introduce intangible/social rewards alongside so he starts to develop a liking for them. Usually it is best to reward a little often rather than a lot occasionally.

Note

There is a behavioural modification system that I have not mentioned here that is commonly used by specialists working with children with AS or other autistic spectrum disorders. It is known as Applied Behaviour Analysis (ABA) and can take a number of forms. Discrete Trial Teaching (DTT) is one of the commonly used modes of ABA. People have had a lot of success with ABA intervention, particularly with children who are more severely autistic; however, it is very time consuming and can be costly. I have not included information about ABA or DTT as you need to learn quite a lot about them before using them. If you wish to learn more about these, there is plenty of material available. If you wish to use them you should discuss them with the appropriate professionals. See the Resources section for further reading.

CHAPTER 4

Can I help the child with his or her social skills?

There are plenty of things you can do to assist with the development of social skills for the child with AS. Whatever you are doing should complement things any other professionals working with the child are doing. Talk with the parents to make sure there is consistency. Some of the strategies already mentioned will help with social skills (e.g. class role), but here are a few more specific ones.

Social stories

One of the tools recognized as most effective for helping to explain and develop understanding of social situations is a social story.

A social story is a technique developed by Carol Gray to help children understand social situations. If you are keen to try these I suggest you read the literature available on them (see the *Further Reading* section at the end of this book). In brief they consist of four types of sentences:

1. *Descriptive* – tells us who is involved, what he or she is doing and where he or she is.

2. *Perspective* – explains the reactions and feelings of the others involved.

3. *Directive* – tells the child what he or she needs to do or say.

4. *Control* – gives the child a way of remembering what to do or say.

There should be a ratio of around five descriptive sentences for every one directive sentence. When writing the stories you have to be very accurate – use words like "usually", "sometimes" and "often" so as to not make the situation too rigid. In the directive sentences avoid words like "must" and "will". Use phrases like "will try to". Here is an example of a social story:

> One of the rooms at school is my classroom (descriptive). The one that is mine at the moment is known as room 8 (descriptive). The same children usually work in room 8 each day (descriptive). A bell rings early in the morning (descriptive). The children know that when the bell rings they have to go to their classroom (perspective). We have to go to our room so that the teacher can help us learn (perspective). When I hear the first bell I will try to go straight to my classroom (directive). Children go straight to classrooms like trains go straight to their stations (control). My teacher will be pleased that I have gone straight to my classroom (perspective).

Comic strip conversations

These are used to illustrate how communication works. They consist of stick figure drawings, simple symbols and colour coding. Pictures are drawn to show a sequence of events. By breaking down a conversation (either actual or hypothetical) and using visual cues, a child can see what is happening, bit by bit.

If you are interested in using this technique, you need to read the relevant literature so that you have an understanding of the symbols and conventions (see *Further Reading* section).

Friendship circles

You can use this pencil and paper technique to explain the different levels of friendship. Start with a small circle with the child's name in. Add a circle around it and put the names of close family members on the circle. Then add another circle around it with the next level of family or friends. You can write between the circles the appropriate way to interact with the various people.

Here is an example of the Friendship Circle. This has been created for a boy called Jack who has been greeting strangers with a kiss and a hug as he does with close family. His name has been placed in the centre. The next circle contains the names of those closest to him. In the bubble is an explanation of how he is to interact with these people. The next circle out is the next closest group of people to him and an explanation of how to interact with them etc. What is placed in the bubbles will de dependant on the child, as will the number of circles and whose names appear in them.

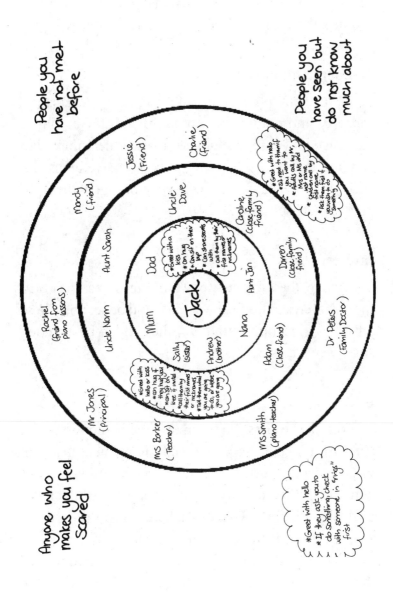

Role play

Go back over situations the student found difficult or stressful using role play. Pause as you go to explain people's thoughts and feelings at various stages.

Openers and closers

Teach the child phrases he can use to start conversation and play, and phrases he can use to end it. Get him to practise with you. Some phrases to use if he is invited to play but doesn't wish to join in would also be useful. Teach him that pauses in a conversation signal the right time to start speaking.

Interest clubs

Encourage the child to join any clubs that relate to special interests she has (or some could be set up). These provide a great opportunity for the child to be included and given status by peers.

Buddies

The rest of the class can be an invaluable support to the child with AS if managed correctly. Remember that you, as the teacher, must model how to respectfully interact with the child. Carefully choose people to be buddies in difficult situations. This can take the form of buddies who work with the child at certain times of the day, buddies to help them in the playground, or buddies for them to go to if they are feeling stressed out. Take the time to talk over with the buddies exactly what you expect of them. Explain why it is that the child needs their support and that they are being trusted with a very important task. Let them know that they can come and see you any time if they don't know what to do. Make sure you check in regularly with the buddies to see how often the child is making use of them and if they need any help. You will need to encourage the child to see these buddies when you first start this. When the child comes to you with something that you think the buddy could help with, ask them if they have asked the buddy first. Always reward the buddies for their good work.

Watching for cues

Other children provide cues as to how to act in any given situation. You can teach the child to watch and take cues from others. Eventually he will be able to use this skill throughout life to help judge what behaviour is appropriate.

When first starting out, explain how you can look at others to see how they are acting. For example, are they silent, talking quietly or running around? Point out children in the class who are good role models that he can look at to see how he should be acting. These children should also be made aware that they will be helping act, particularly as they may get stared at intensely for the first few days!

Discuss why you are choosing these particular children. Tell the child with AS that some children know the best way to behave more than others. A child with AS can easily be led astray, so this step is very important.

TV programs

This activity is more easily done at home. If you choose to do it at school, then it needs to be done one-on-one.

Prerecord TV programs such as 3rd Rock From The Sun and Mr Bean, where characters act in a different manner from what is generally acceptable. Explain that you will be watching a fun program where characters do funny things. Watch a segment of the video with the child. Rewind and watch it again but this time pause the video when the characters do something that is inappropriate. Talk about what is inappropriate and discuss what they could have done instead.

Be careful that this activity does not make the child more self-conscious. Keep the session light-hearted and have a laugh at the silly things that are done.

Prompts

If the child is going to be required to talk to someone he is unfamiliar with (e.g. a student teacher, visiting researcher), someone responsible can stand beside the child and whisper suggestions of what to say in the child's ear.

Exploring emotions

Once a week, spend a little time studying an emotion. Brainstorm when the emotion occurs, what the cues are, how people act and some phrases to use to express this emotion. This is an activity that can be beneficial to the whole class. The child may actually learn more from other children's answers. Spending some time one-on-one with the child afterwards, recapping what is discussed, will help to reinforce the learning.

Topic talking times

Often other children do not wish to hear about the child's special interest every day. It can help to tell the child to avoid talking about the special topic in the playground and instead set up a particular time when he can talk about this topic with an adult. Alternatively, teach the child the signs to watch out for that indicate when a person has heard enough. This can be particularly difficult, as a child will often forget about everything else as he starts to talk about his special interest.

Bullying

The points covered in this chapter and in the previous one on social skills will all help children with AS to avoid becoming a victim of bullying. Unfortunately their lack of social understanding and motor skills makes them stick out in the playground. Combine this with their inability to understand someone else's motivations and you have a prime target for bullying. Is there anything else you can do?

Bullying is often drastically reduced if the child is not isolated in the playground. Therefore the buddy system discussed earlier in the chapter will help out here. A person that is keeping an eye out for them or someone they can go for help will assist greatly. However, there is no substitute for real friends and although a buddy may develop into a friend, this does not happen automatically. What we need to do is help friendships to form.

To do this, many people make the mistake of finding another child with AS, putting the two of them together and calling them friends. In fact in this situation they are even less likely to become friends, as neither knows quite what they are supposed to do. Just think how you would react if you were placed with a another person just because they have the same hair colour as you and were told that you should be friends! A far more successful method is to use interest clubs or to foster any small friendships you see naturally forming, as discussed in the social skills chapter. Friendship is usually based upon shared interests so you are going to have the most success if you spot the child interacting with another child with similar interests and encourage the two to do something together based upon those interests.

Above all else, the staff in the school need to be made aware of the child's vulnerability. This is because it is hard to spot the most common form of bullying a child with AS will be subjected to. Other children will soon learn that they can tell the child with AS to do or say things and that child will happily go and do or say them. Other children only need to pretend that they are being friendly and the child with AS will take what they say to be completely true. At the other children's suggestion the child with AS will then unwittingly go along and break school rules or act inappropriately. A teacher will spot this and the child will be in trouble and be completely confused as to why. Staff need to be trained to look beyond what they see the child with AS doing, to what caused them to do it, and deal with that aspect firmly.

CHAPTER 5

How can I help the child in the playground?

The playground is probably the most threatening environment you could put a child with AS into. Vast open spaces, complex social interactions, a myriad of unwritten rules to adhere to, and a plethora of sounds, sights and smells combine to make a child with AS feel at a loss. It is also a situation in which a child with AS who has poor motor skills will stand out like a sore thumb and be particularly vulnerable to bullying, both physical and verbal.

Many of the skills discussed in the social skills chapter will aid the child in coping in the playground environment. In addition, here are a few more tips.

- Have places where the child can go if it all becomes too much.

- Identify who the child can go to for help if he or she needs it.

- Encourage any positive friendships you see developing.

- Consider arranging for the child a mix of the first half of lunch in the playground and the second half in a quiet place (e.g. library). This will help the child relax and prepare him or herself for the afternoon's work.

- Make sure other staff are properly informed about Asperger Syndrome and the implications for the child so they can keep an eye on things.

- Talk to the child about the difference between teasing and joking. What cues are there that a person is doing one or the other? Teach him how to respond appropriately.

- Use the teacher aide in the playground rather than solely in the classroom. They can help the child make sense of it all and coach him through social situations.

CHAPTER 6

What should the teacher aide be focusing on?

Ideally you will be able to secure some teacher aide time for the child. Explore as many avenues for funding as you can. The teacher aide should always be working to help the child become more independent and be teaching her coping strategies, rather than becoming someone the child relies on and who rescues her. If that is kept in mind, then the teacher aide will always be beneficial. Things they could do include:

- Showing the child how to get her things organized for the day.

- Helping the child invent a system for keeping her possessions organized.

- Encouraging the child to be social, flexible and co-operative in various situations.

- Spotting ways of using the child's special interest to motivate her to do class work.

- Helping her understand the unwritten rules of social interaction by using comic strip conversations or discussing situations with the child explaining what other people may be thinking, or what leads them to do certain things.

- Writing social stories to aid the child's understanding of feelings and friendships (may need training to do this effectively).

- Encouraging her to talk with others. Be the prompt that whispers in her ear suggestions of what to say.

- Doing exercises prescribed by professional support people to improve motor skills.

- Giving extra tuition in areas of difficulty.

- Showing the child ways of dealing with sensory sensitivity (see Chapter 3).

Where possible get the teacher aide to work with the child both individually and as part of a group made up of a *cross section* of the class. This is important for the child's self-esteem.

CHAPTER 7

Who else in the school needs to know?

This is a sensitive issue that needs to be discussed with the parents. Ask yourself, "Will it help this person if they know that this child has AS"? If the answer is yes, then it is probably a good idea to tell them. It is useful for all staff that have regular contact with the child to have an understanding of AS so they do not misinterpret the child's actions and can be supportive. The issue is further complicated if the child does not yet know that he or she has AS. In the end it is the parents' decision. Talk the issue over with them.

People react in different ways to being told someone has a condition like AS. Make sure that collagues are accurately (and adequately) informed about the syndrome so as to discourage them from acting in the following ways:

- Putting the diagnosis down to an excuse for poor behaviour using the latest psychobabble.

- Using the diagnosis as an excuse to exclude the child from activities rather than finding ways to include him or her.

- Confusing the diagnosis with other conditions.

- Spreading the news around and discussing it openly without regard for the child or his or her family.

Two other issues with disclosure also arise. The first is how to tell the class that a child has AS and the second is how to work with a child if they do not know that they have AS. Both can be solved using the same strategy.

Arrange a time to talk with the class about different learning styles. Discuss how some people like to work in lots of noise and some with none, how some like skipping around books quickly and some like reading from start to finish, and how some people like things to change and be different all the time and some like things always to remain the same. Even young children seem to grasp this concept well.

You can create a chart with all the different ways people like to learn and all the different learning environments that people find helpful. With older children you can even get them to identify what they think works best for them and display these on a wall. This will help the children in the class be more tolerant of each other and provides you with a way of relating AS to the class.

After completing this exercise, when you need to work with a child who does not know he has AS, you can explain that you are using certain strategies because of his unique learning style, which of course is true! He will be able to relate to this and will already know that everyone has unique learning styles – not just him. Children that know they have AS can also benefit from looking at it in this manner, particularly if they are self-conscious about having AS. You will most likely find, however, that they are comfortable with their diagnosis. Most already realize they are different and experience relief more than anything at finding out it is due to having AS.

If you find yourself needing to tell the class that the child has AS (and you have discussed this with the parents) then you can relate AS to learning styles. You can describe how this child's learning style is extremely important to him and that he finds it really hard to use a different style. You can describe how he likes his learning environment set up in a certain way and need things to be logical and structured.

Reading a children's book on Asperger Syndrome can also be helpful here. A good one is *Blue Bottle Mystery* (and its sequels) by Kathy Hoopman (see Resources section).

CHAPTER 8

Should I make the child do homework?

Children with AS tend to view school as the place to work, and home as the place to relax. Any suggestion to do work at home can cause great stress. Why should he be working at his place of rest? In addition, the strategies and interventions used at school to aid the child in his or her work may not be available at home. It is therefore really important that you discuss this topic with the child's parents at the earliest opportunity.

The issue of homework is further compounded by the fact that most children with AS require more "down time" than their peers to recover from the day at school. They have been working twice as hard as the other students. Not only have they been doing all the school work, they have also been trying hard to decipher social situations, confusing statements, body language and facial expressions; they have been coping with huge amounts of sensory stimulation and have been trying to adjust to unexpected changes in their routines. By the time school ends they are often physically and mentally exhausted. On top of all this, the child will often still be processing events from the day and will need time for his mind to "wind down" so he can concentrate on something new.

With all these factors in mind, the question that needs to be asked is, "Is the gain made from doing homework worth the amount of stress that is caused?" In situations of low stress the answer will be "yes", but in many cases the ongoing battle may not be worth it.

Modifying the Homework Environment

Let us look at the case where homework is difficult but not causing huge amounts of stress. In this situation, the homework environment needs to be modified to make the work as easy as possible for the child.

First of all, the child needs to choose a place with his parents that will be his homework spot. The child should never be required to do homework outside of this place. It should be free from any distraction. Take time to think about sensory issues. For example, are there noises that will upset him?

Set definite start and end times to the homework with scheduled break time in between. Create a reward system that is linked to the amount of work done in this time, not to how quickly he does a certain piece of work. This stops homework becoming never ending for both the child and the parents. Help him by prioritizing the work so that the most important tasks will be done first.

The need to handwrite work can add extra pressure. It often takes a large amount of concentration to write legibly and therefore the child's focus is moved from their work to their writing. Having a computer available in the place of work and making it possible to word process at least part of the homework may help.

Modifying the Homework Structure

If homework is causing a large amount of stress then more creative solutions need to be found.

Make sure all your homework instructions are written down. If you just give them verbally or add key information verbally to written instructions, the child is likely to be confused or not be able to remember it all.

You, as the teacher, need to look through the homework that you set and decide what is really going to be of benefit to the child. Prioritize tasks and remove ones that are not going to be of much benefit. If you can, alter the main tasks so that they are more appealing to the child. For example, consider the case where a teacher is setting a research assignment on sea life. If the primary objective is for the child to practise researching then why can't he do research on one of his special interests instead? Conversely, if the primary objective is learning about sea life, can he read some books on the subject or watch a movie about it (two easier tasks) instead?

Tasks that are going to take more than one night to complete will most likely need monitoring. She could easily become confused at the beginning of the process and go off on a completely different tangent. She could bring her work to you after completing her initial plan and at each key stage for checking. At this point you should go over the expectations for the next stage again.

If he is having real difficulty with the concept of doing work at home, investigate other places he could go to do it. Perhaps he could have a small break then work in the library after school. Is there a family member's place that he will find it easier to work at?

Remember too that he may just be too exhausted to work after school. Is he actually going to benefit from doing homework in this case? Are there some essential tasks in the homework that he could do during another part of the school day? For example during library time, spare periods, or part of the lunch time.

Tony Attwood has written an excellent paper on this issue. I suggest that you visit the website www.tony attwood.com to read it, and draw it to the attention of the child's parent and discuss it with them if possible.

Luke Jackson (a teenager with AS) provides a very good explanation of homework from the point of view of the child with AS in his book *Freaks, Geeks and Asperger Syndrome*. It is well worth a read and will help you understand your student's way of viewing the world. See the Further Reading Section.

CHAPTER 9

How can the child be assisted with study?

As the child gets older, he or she is going to have to learn how to study independently and needs to be taught strategies for this. Here are some general study skills tips that will help any child, but particularly one with AS.

- Set up a place where the study will happen. It will need to have good lighting and be free from distractions.

- Set definite start and end times for the study session. Schedule breaks at regular intervals.

- Start with the least favourite subject first.

- Put in place goals for how much work will be done. The child can choose rewards he will give himself for achieving the goals.

- Show him how to use colour when note taking, by colour coding different ideas and highlighting the key concepts.

- Show him how to organize his work so that notes for different subjects are kept in different books.

- Get him to attach a plastic sleeve to each book where any loose notes or handouts can be placed.

- Allow him to spend some time on his favourite hobby or special interest if he becomes overwhelmed.

- Experiment with soothing music to see if it helps the study.

- Have something for the child to hold and squeeze when reading over material e.g. stress ball, Blue-Tac, sponge.

- Get him to draw pictures of concepts to help him remember.

- Get him started then leave him to it for a little while. He can check with you after each section.

CHAPTER 10

What should happen before the child changes class or school?

Children with Asperger Syndrome resist change in most aspects of their lives before they find it incredibly stressful. A change of class, therefore, and even more so a change of school, are going to be especially stressful due to the scale of change. If you can do the following, you will ease the transition.

- Get the new teacher to come and observe your classroom. He or she can pick up on strategies and routines that are working well in your class.

- If possible make sure the new teacher meets the child with AS more than once before the necessary transition.

- Make yourself available as a resource person for the new teacher. Pass on tips and tricks.

- Organize for the child to visit the new class or school. Point out major landmarks that he or she can use to orientate him or herself.

Have lots of these visits and schedule them for different times of the day so the child can see different things happening.

• If actual visits are not possible, get a photo book made up. This can include pictures of important places in the school, the members of staff, and routines in action.

• If going to a new school where the child will have more than one teacher (e.g. college) then make sure one teacher is appointed to monitor the transition.

• Organize for the staff at the school to have a brief introduction to AS during a staff meeting.

• See whether you can arrange a period of overlap with the existing and new support staff so everyone has time to learn and adjust.

CHAPTER 11

Am I qualified to teach this child?

The age and experience of the teacher, prior experience with AS and additional qualifications have only a small impact on the teacher's ability actually to teach a child with AS. What is far more important is that the teacher is calm, predictable and flexible. You as the teacher need to maintain a good sense of humour and be prepared to ask for help whenever you need it. Be forever looking for the positives in the child and ensure your classroom is a place of encouragement, not criticism. Anyone can teach a child with AS, so long as they have the right attitude. Enjoy sharing in the child's unique view of the world.

CHAPTER 12

I want to know more – where should I start?

I have listed the references I have used at the back of the book. The full reference for any book I mention in this section can be found there.

If I could only recommend two books that I have read at the time of publishing, they would have to be Tony Attwood's book entitled *Asperger's Syndrome: A Guide For Parents and Professionals* and the *OASIS Guide to Asperger's Syndrome.* Tony Attwood's book has comprehensive information in easy to read language and the OASIS guide has large amounts of extra background information on a wide variety of areas to do with AS. Both these books are linked to excellent websites. Tony Attwood's site also contains the paper he wrote about homework. Both are wonderful springboards for finding more information:

> *www.tonyattwood.com*

> *www.udel.edu/bkirby/asperger*

If you are having specific issues with the child in your class then *Asperger Syndrome – Practical Strategies for the*

Classroom by George Thomas, Phil Whitaker, Penny Barratt, Heather Clewley, Helen Joy and Mo Potter could be very useful. It is organized by areas of difficulty. You look up the specific section on what you or the child are having trouble with. Each section contains a brief example of the difficulty, some reasons it occurs and a couple of strategies that help with it. A great Canadian website that has a list of strategies matched up with particular difficulties is: *www.sasked. gov.sk.ca/k/pecs/se/docs/autism/asper.html*

The other type of book to explore is one written by someone with AS. *Pretending to be Normal* by Liane Holliday Willey, talks about what it has been like growing up with AS. *Asperger Syndrome, the Universe and Everything* by Kenneth Hall is an insightful little book written by a child coming to terms with AS. *Freaks, Geeks and Asperger Syndrome: A User Guide To Adolescence* by Luke Jackson is a witty and insightful book by a teenager with AS. He cleverly balances explaining his experiences of AS to the general reader with tips and pieces of wisdom for other teens with AS. A particularly good book for teenagers with AS to read themselves. All three are fascinating reads and I am sure there are plenty more similar books out there. To understand the struggle parents go through try *Eating an Artichoke* by Echo R. Fling. In particular, it provides insights on the struggles with educational placement.

One of the best books on visual strategies that can be used in a classroom is *Visual Strategies for Improving*

Communication by Linda A. Hodgdon. It contains plenty of practical ideas with examples.

Most countries have Autism Associations that will be able to provide you with more specific information and support. A growing number also have organizations dedicated to Asperger Syndrome. Some contact details for these organizations follow.

USA

Autism Society of America
Phone: 1 800 3AUTISM
Or ++1 301 657 0881
Post: 7910 Woodmont Avenue
Suite 300
Bethesda
Maryland 20814-3067
U.S.A.
Email: membership@autism-society.org
Website: www.autism-society.org

Asperger Syndrome Coalition of the US
Phone: 1 866 4ASPRGR
Post: PO Box 351268
Jacksonville, FL 32235-1268
Website: www.asperger.org

UK

National Autistic Society
Phone: ++44 20 7833 2299
Post: 393 City Road
London EC1V 1NG
UK
Email: nas@nas.org.nz
Website: www.nas.org.uk

CANADA

Autism Society Canada
Phone: 1 866 874 3334
Or ++1 519 942 8720
Post: P.O. Box 65,
Orangeville, ON L9W 2Z5
Canada
Email: info@autismsocietycanada.ca
Website: www.autismsocietycanada.ca

AUSTRALIA

Agencies in Australia are state based but the following one can put you in contact with the other organisations:

Autism Victoria
Phone: ++61 3 9885 0533
Post: PO Box 235
Ashburton
Victoria
Australia 3147
Email: admin@autismvictoria.org.au
Website: www.autismvictoria.org.au

And of course there is the **Cloud 9 Children's Foundation** in New Zealand who commissioned the writing of this booklet:
Phone: ++64 4 920 9473
Post: PO Box 30979
Lower Hutt
Wellington
New Zealand
Email: foundation@entercloud9.com
Website: www.withyoueverystepoftheway.com

I hope you have many enjoyable experiences teaching a child with AS and come to recognize the special gifts that they have.

Further reading

Attwood, T. (1998) *Asperger's Syndrome: A Guide for Parents and Professionals.* London: Jessica Kingsley Publishers.

Jackson, L. (2002) *Freaks, Geeks and Asperger's Syndrome: A User Guide to Adolescence.* London: Jessica Kingsley Publishers.

Wiley, L.H. (1999) *Pretending to be Normal: Living with Asperger's Syndrome.* London: Jessica Kingsley Publishers.

Moyes, R.A. (2001) *Incorporating Social Goals in the Classroom: A Guide for Teachers and Parents of Children with High-Functioning Autism and Asperger Syndrome.* London: Jessica Kingsley Publishers.

Moyes, R.A. (2002) *Addressing the Challenging Behaviour of Children with High-Functioning Autism/Asperger Syndrome in the Classroom: A Guide for Teachers and Parents.* London: Jessica Kingsley Publishers.

References

Attwood, T. (1998) *Asperger's Syndrome: A Guide for Parents and Professionals*. London: Jessica Kingsley Publishers.

Attwood, T. (April 2000) 'Should Children with an Autistic Spectrum Disorder be Exempted From Doing Homework?', Academic Paper. *www.tonyattwood.com*

Burgoine, E. and Wing, L. (1983) 'Identical triplets with Asperger's Syndrome.' In *British Journal of Psychiatry, 143.*

Edelson, S. (1995) 'Theory of Mind', Academic Paper written for Center for the Study of Autism, Salem, Oregon. *http://www.autism.org/mind.html*

Fling E. R. (2000) *Eating an Artichoke: A Mother's Perspective on Asperger's Syndrome.* London: Jessica Kingsley Publishers.

Grandin, T. (June 2001) 'Teaching Tips for Children and Adults with Autism', Academic Paper. *http://www.autism. org/temple/tips.html*

Gray, C. (1994) *Comic Strip Conversations.* Arlington: Future Horizons.

Gray, C. (1997) *Social Stories and Comic Strip Conversations. Unique Methods To Improve Social Understanding.* Jenison, Michigan: The Morning News.

Hall, K. (2000) *Asperger Syndrome, the Universe and Everything.* London: Jessica Kingsley Publishers.

Holliday Willey, L. (1999) *Pretending to be Normal: Living with Asperger's Syndrome.* London: Jessica Kingsley Publishers.

Hoopmann, K. (2001) *Blue Bottle Mystery: An Asperger Adventure.* London: Jessica Kingsley Publishers.

Ives, M. (1999) 'What is Asperger Syndrome and How Will It Affect Me: A Guide For Young People.' London: National Autistic Society.

Jackel, S. (June 1996) 'Asperger's Syndrome – Educational Management Issues', Academic Paper. *http://members. ozemail.com.au/prussia/asperger/teach.htm*

Kirby, B. and Romanwski, P. (2001) *The OASIS Guide to Asperger Syndrome.* Arlington: Future Horizons.

Leicester City Council Education Department and Leicestershire County Council Education Department (1998) 'Asperger Syndrome – Practical Strategies for the Classroom: A Teacher's Guide.' London: The National Autistic Society.

Websites

O.A.S.I.S.
www.udel.edu/bkirb/asperger/ or *www.aspergersyndrome.org/*

Tony Attwood
www.tonyattwood.com

Cloud 9 Children's Foundation
www.withyoueverystepoftheway.com

Educating the Student With Asperger Syndrome
www.sasked.gov.sk.ca/k/pecs/se/docs/autism/asper.html

Centre for the Study of Autism
www.autism.org

Asperger Syndrome Education Network
www.aspennj.org

Asperger Information Page
www.aspergerinfo.freeservers.com

Asperger's Disorder Homepage
www.aspergers.com

ASPEN (Asperger Syndrome Education Network)
www.asperger.org

Families of Adults Afflicted with Asperger Syndrome
www.faaas.org

Asperger Syndrome for Parents, Professionals and Educators
www.aspergersyndrome.com

Oops – Wrong Planet!
www.isn.net/-jypsy

Autism Resource Site
www.autism-resources.com

Ben's Asperger Room
www.asperger-syndrome.com

Resources

Applied Behaviour Analysis

Leaf, R., McEachin, J., Harsh, J. and Boehm, M. (1999) *A Work in Progress: Behavior Management Strategies & A Curriculum for Intensive Behavioral Treatment of Autism.* New York: DRL Books.

Maurice, C., Green, G. and Luce, S. (1996) *Behavioral Intervention for Young Children With Autism: A Manual for Parents and Professionals.* Austin, TX: Pro Ed.

Newman, B., Reinecke, D., Birch, S., and Blausten, F. (2002) *Graduated Applied Behavior Analysis.* Dove and Orca.

Classroom Activities For Children with AS

Davalos, S. (1999) *Making Sense of Art: Sensory-Based Art Activities for Children with Autism, Asperger Syndrome and Pervasive Developmental Disorders Autism.* Shawnee Mission, KS: Autism Asperger Publishing Company.

Faherty, C. (2000) *Asperger's: What Does It Mean to Me?* Arlington, TX: Future Horizons.

Moyes, R. (2002) *Addressing the Challenging Behavior of Children with High-Functioning Autism/Asperger Syndrome in the Classroom: A Guide for Teachers and Parents.* London: Jessica Kingsley Publishers.

Moyes, R. (2001) *Incorporating Social Goals in the Classroom: A Guide for Teachers and Parents of Children with High-Functioning Autism and Asperger Syndrome.* London: Jessica Kingsley Publishers.

Fiction

Hoopman, K. (2000) *Blue Bottle Mystery: An Asperger Adventure.* London: Jessica Kingsley Publishers.

Hoopman, K. (2001) *Of Mice and Aliens: An Asperger Adventure.* London: Jessica Kingsley Publishers.

Hoopman, K. (2002) *Lisa and the Lacemaker: An Asperger Adventure.* London: Jessica Kingsley Publishers.

Hoopman, K. (2003) *Haze.* London: Jessica Kingsley Publishers.

Nichol, T. (2003) *Stephen Harris in Trouble: A Dyspraxic Drama in Several Clumsy Acts.* London: Jessica Kingsley Publishers.

Ogaz, N. (2002) *Buster and the Amazing Daisy.* London: Jessica Kingsley Publishers.

Social Stories

Gray, C. and White, A. (2002) *My Social Stories Book.* London: Jessica Kingsley Publishers.

Visual Stratagies

Bromley, K., Irwin-De Vitis, L. and Modlo, M. (1995) *Graphic Organizers: Visual Strategies for Active Learning.* New York: Scholastic, Inc.

Hodgdon, L.A. (1995) *Visual Strategies for Improving Communication: Practical Supports for School and Home.* Troy, MI: Quirk Roberts Publishing.

McClannahan, L. and Krantz, P. (1999) *Activity Schedules for Children with Autism: Teaching Independent Behaviour (Topics in Autism).* Bethesda, MD: Woodbine House.

Savner, J. and Myles, B. (2000) *Making Visual Supports Work in the Home and Community: Strategies for Individuals with Autism and Asoerger Syndrome.* Shawnee Mission, KS: Autism Asperger Publsihing Company.

Tarquin, P. and Walker, S. (1996) *Creating Success in the Classroom: Bisual Organizers and How to Use Them.* Westport, CT: Libraries Unlimited.

Some Common Conditions Associated with Asperger Syndrome

ADD/ADHD (Attention Deficit Disorder/Attention Deficit Hyperactivity Disorder)

Flick, G.L. (1997) *ADD/ADHD Behavior-Change Resource Kit: Ready-to-Use Strategies & Activities for Helping Children with Attention Deficit Disorder.* San Francisco: Jossey-Bass Publishers.

Holowenko, H. (1994) *Attention Deficit/Hyperactivity Disorder: A Multidisciplinary Approach.* London: Jessica Kingsley Publishers.

Levine, M. (2002) *A Mind at a Time.* New York: Simon & Schuster Publishers.

Munden, A. and Arcelus, J. (1999) *The ADHD Handbook: A Guide for Parents and Professionals.* London: Jessica Kingsley Publishers.

Dysgraphia

Cavey, D.W. (2000) *Dysgraphia: Why Johnny Can't Write: A Handbook for Teachers and Parents (3rd Edition).* Austin, TX: Pro-Ed Publishers.

Olsen, J.Z. (1998) *Handwriting Without Tears (Teachers edition, 7th Edition)* Potomac, MD: Handwriting Without Tears Publishers.

Dyslexia

McCabe, D. (1997) *To Teach A Dyslexic.* Clio, MI: AVKO Educational Research.

Ryden, M. (1997) *Dyslexia: How Would I Cope? (3rd Edition).* London: Jessica Kingsley Publishers.

Stowe, C.M. (2000) *How to Reach and Teach Children and Teens With Dyslexia: A Parent and Teacher Guide to Helping All Ages Academically, Socially, and Emotionally.* San Francisco: Jossey-Bass Publishers.

Dyspraxia

Ball, M.F. (2002) *Developmental Coordination Disorder: Hints and Tips for the Activities of Daily Living.* London: Jessica Kingsley Publishers.

Boon, M. (2000) *Helping Children with Dyspraxia.* London: Jessica Kingsley Publishers.

Portwood, M. (1999) *Developmental Dyspraxia - Identification and Intervention: A Manual for Parents and Professionals (2nd Edition).* London: David Fulton Publishers.

Echolalia / Tourette Syndrome

Dornbush, M.P. and Pruitt, S.K.(1995) *Teaching the Tiger: A Handbook for Individuals Involved in the Education of Students with Attention Deficit Disorders, Tourette Syndrome or Obsessive-Compulsive Disorder.* Duarte, CA: Hope Press.

Robertson, M.M. and Baron-Cohen, S. (1998) *Tourette Syndrome: The Facts.* Oxford: Oxford University Press.

Shimberg, E.F. (1995) *Living With Tourette Syndrome.* New York: Simon and Schuster Publishers.

NLD (Nonverbal Learning Disability)

Anderson, W., Chitwood, S. and Hayden, D. (1990) *Negotiating the Special Education Maze: A Guide for Parents and Teachers.* Bethesda, MD: Woodbine House.

Tanguay, P.B. (2002) *Nonverbal Learning Disabilities at School: Educating Students with NLD, Asperger Syndrome and Related Conditions.* London: Jessica Kingsley Publishers.

Thompson, S. (1997) *The Source for Nonverbal Learning Disorders* (formally titled I Shouldn't Have to Tell You! A Guide to Understanding Nonverbal Learning Disorders). East Moline, IL: LinguiSystems Inc.á.

OCD (Obsessive Compulsive Disorder)

Hyman, B.M. and Pedrick, C. (1999) *The OCD Workbook: Your Guide to Breaking Free from Obsessive-Compulsive Disorder.* Oakland, CA: New Harbinger Publishers.

Thomsen, P.H. (1999) *From Thoughts to Obsessions: Obsessive Compulsive Disorder in Children and Adolescents.* London: Jessica Kingsley Publishers.

Waltz, M. and Claiborn, J.M. (2000) *Obsession Compulsive Disorder: Help for Children and Adolescents.* Cambridge, MA: Patient-Centered Guides, A Division of O'Reilly & Associates, Inc.

Index